Christmas
is not all about Presents

Written and Illustrated
by Lu Hebb

Printed in the United States of America

First Printing, 2017.

ISBN-13: 978-1981527175
ISBN-10: 1981527176

for Olivia and Ava

Christmas is just around the corner!

It's a lot of decorations.

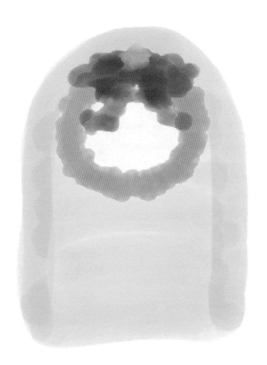

But it's not all about decorations.

Although **decorating is fun**.

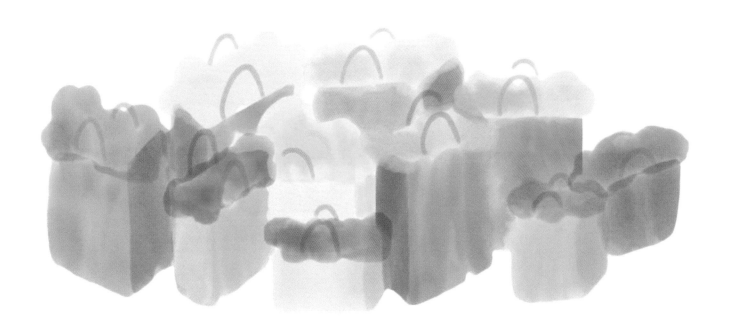

It's a lot of shopping.

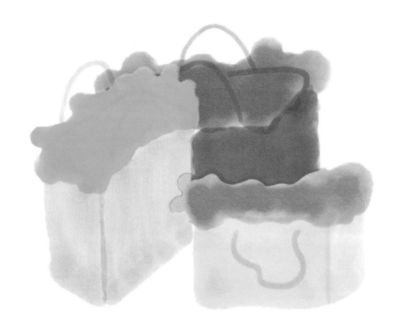

But it's not all about shopping.

Although **shopping for someone we want to give presents to is fun**.

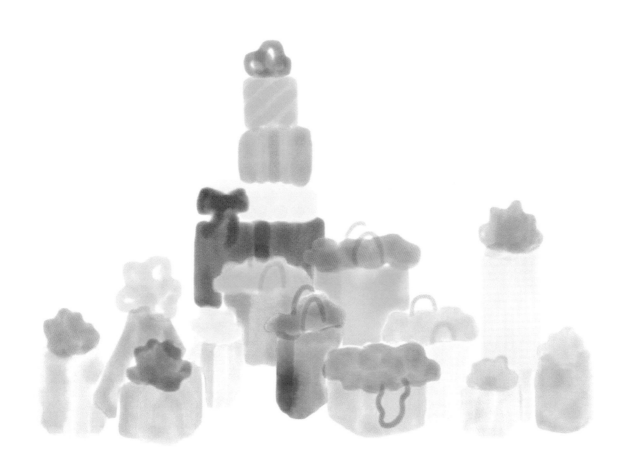

It's a lot of presents.

But it's not all about presents.

Although we all **love the presents we receive**.

It's a lot of Christmas cards.

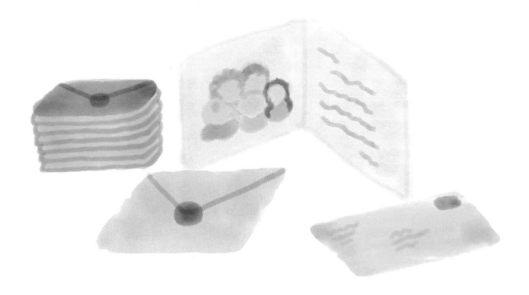

But it's not all about Christmas cards.

Although we **like to see the pictures of families and friends**,
especially when they live far away.

It's a lot of Christmas trees.

But it's not all about Christmas trees.

Although we like the **twinkling lights** and we like to

see the number of ornaments on the tree grow every year.

Christmas songs are everywhere.

But it's not all about Christmas songs.

Although we like to listen to them and **feel merry**.

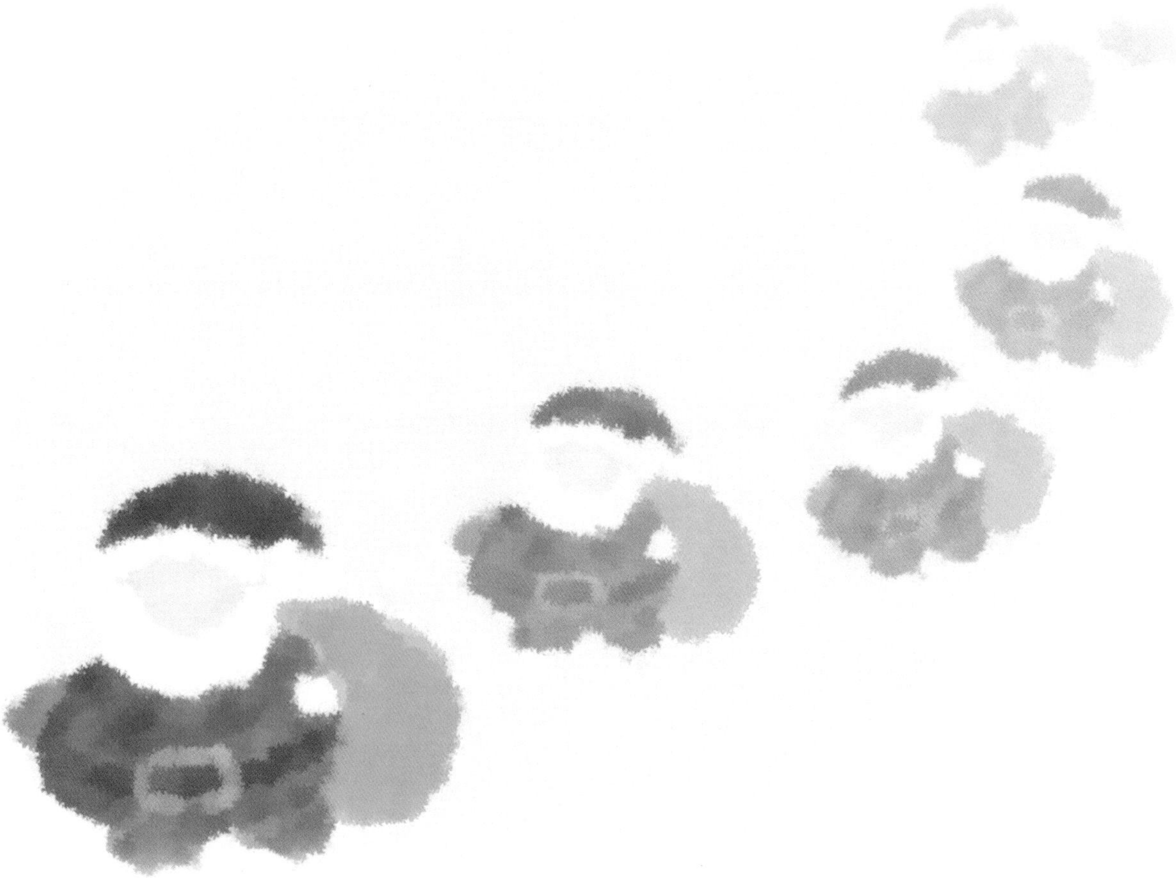

Santa is busy going everywhere.

But it's not all about Santa.

Although we don't want him to miss our house,
and **he will be sure to come**,
even on the coldest snowy Christmas Eve.

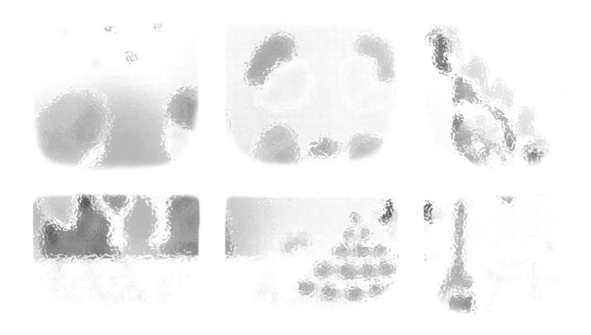

Friends and families are busy partying
and making big dinners.

But it's not all about parties and dinners.

Although we **enjoy gathering** and
eating **delicious food**.

Then, what's **Christmas actually** about?

It's actually Jesus' birthday

that we all **celebrate with love** and **hope**.

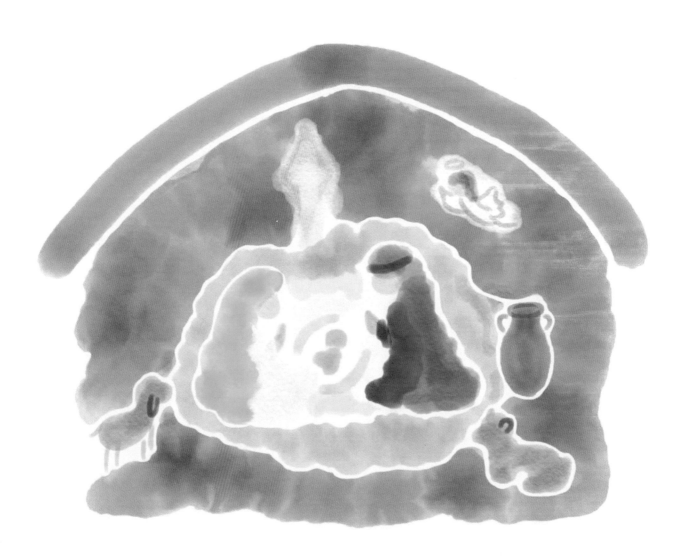

It's what we are **looking forward to**,

when the leaves start turning colors and the weather gets cold.

It fills the air with the **aroma**

of homemade dishes.

It's when we all receive presents and feel **surprised**,

no matter big or small.

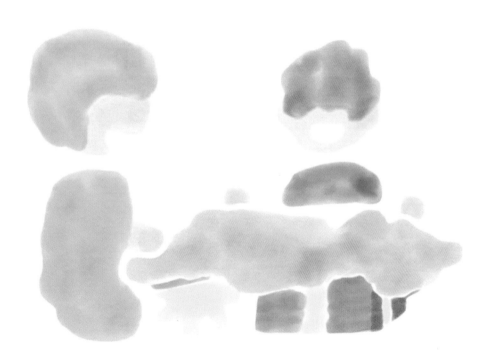

It's time when we greet the ones

we don't see often,

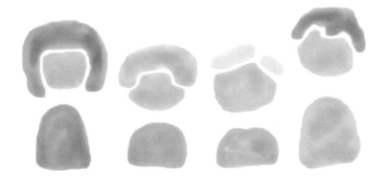

but we **care** so dearly about.

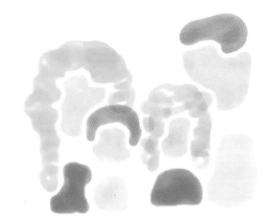

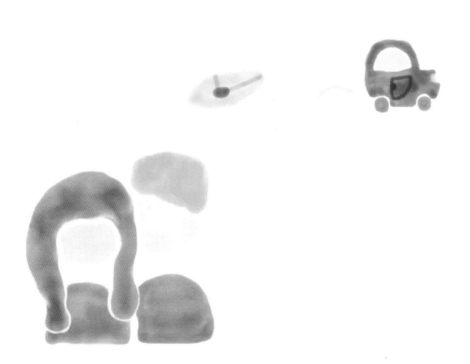

It's **grandmas** and **grandpas**
smiling and opening arms to their grandchildren.

It's time **moms** and **dads**
cuddle with their children throughout the day.

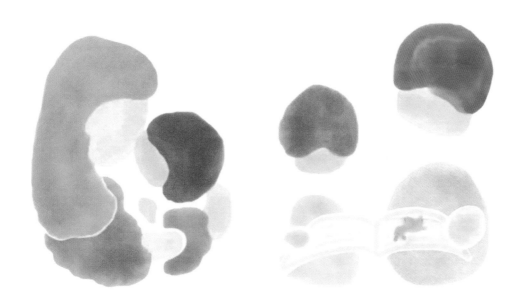

Christmas

It's all about
family.

It's all about
being with our loved ones.

It's all about

feeling **hope** and

looking forward to the **New Year**.

Merry Christmas!

Be merry with your family and your loved ones!

Made in the USA
Columbia, SC
03 February 2018